45

THEMATIC UNIT
Magnets

Written by Jennifer Overend Prior, M. Ed.

Teacher Created Materials, Inc.
6421 Industry Way
Westminster, CA 92683
www.teachercreated.com
©1999 Teacher Created Materials, Inc.
Made in U.S.A.
ISBN-1-57609-377-X

Illustrator:
Howard Chaney

Editor:
Janet A. Hale, M.S. Ed.

Cover Artist:
Cheri Macoubrie Wilson

Table of Contents

Introduction

Magnets is a captivating, comprehensive thematic unit. Its 80 exciting pages are filled with a wide variety of lesson ideas designed for use with primary children. At its core are two high-quality children's literature selections, *Marta's Magnets* and *What Makes a Magnet?* For these books, activities are included which set the stage for reading, encourage the enjoyment of the book, and extend the concepts gained. In addition, the theme is connected to the curriculum with activities in language arts (including daily writing suggestions), math, science, social studies, art, music, and movement. Many of these activities encourage cooperative learning. Suggestions and patterns for bulletin boards and unit-management tools are additional time savers for the busy teacher. Furthermore, directions for child-created Big Books and culminating activities are included, which allows children to synthesize their knowledge.

This thematic unit includes:

❑ **literature selections**—summaries of two children's books with related lessons (complete with reproducible pages) that cross the curriculum

❑ **poetry**—suggested selections and a poem outline enabling children to write and publish their own works

❑ **planning guides**—suggestions for sequencing lessons each day of the unit

❑ **writing ideas**—daily suggestions as well as writing activities across the curriculum, including a big book

❑ **bulletin board ideas**—suggestions and plans for child-created and/or interactive bulletin boards

❑ **curriculum connections**—in language arts, math, science, social studies, art, music, and movement

❑ **group projects**—to foster cooperative learning

❑ **a culminating activity**—which require children to synthesize their learning to produce a product or engage in an activity that can be shared with others

> **To keep this valuable resource intact so that it can be used year after year, you may wish to punch holes in the pages and store them in a three-ring binder.**

Introduction *(cont.)*

Why A Balanced Approach?

The strength of a balanced language approach is that it involves children in using all modes of communication—reading, writing, listening, illustrating, and doing. Communication skills are interconnected and integrated into lessons that emphasize the whole of language. Implicit in this approach is our knowledge that every whole—including individual words—is composed of parts, and directed study of those parts can help a child to master the whole. Experience and research tell us that regular attention to phonics, other word attack skills, spelling, etc., develops reading mastery, thereby fulfilling the unity of the whole language experience. The child is thus led to read, write, spell, speak, and listen more confidently.

Why Thematic Planning?

One very useful tool for implementing an integrated language program is thematic planning. By choosing a theme with a correlating literature selection for a unit of study, a teacher can plan activities throughout the day that lead to a cohesive, in-depth study of the topic. Children will be practicing and applying their skills in meaningful context. Consequently, they tend to learn and retain more.

Why Cooperative Learning?

Besides academic skills and content, children need to learn social skills. No longer can this area of development be taken for granted. Children must learn to work cooperatively in groups in order to function well in modern society. Group activities should be a regular part of school life and teachers should consciously include social objectives as well as academic objectives in their planning.

Why Big Books?

An excellent cooperative, whole language activity is the production of Big Books. Groups of children, or the whole class, can apply their language skills, content knowledge, and creativity to produce a big book that becomes a part of the classroom library to be read and reread. These books make excellent culminating projects for sharing beyond the classroom with parents, librarians, other classes, etc.

Why Journals?

Each day your children should have the opportunity to write in a journal. They may respond to a book or an event in history, write about a personal experience, or answer a general "question of the day" posed by the teacher. The cumulative journal provides an excellent means of documenting children's writing progress.

Marta's Magnets

by Wendy Pfeffer

Summary

Marta likes to collect things. Her favorite collection is an assortment of magnets. Marta discovers that her magnets help her make friends with children in her neighborhood. Her new friends are fascinated with all the things magnets can do. Marta's magnets save the day when a neighbor girl drops her house key through a grate in the street.

Sample Plan

Lesson I

- Discuss the concept of collections (page 6, Setting the Stage, #3).
- Complete Collectors' Graphs (page 40).
- Read *Marta's Magnets*.
- Conduct Magnetic Attractions (page 43).
- Discuss Magnets At Home and School (page 9).
- Sing the Little Magnet song (page 62).
- Select a Daily Writing Activity (pages 34 and 35).

Lesson II

- Reread or review *Marta's Magnets*.
- Enjoy the Jumprope Rhymes (page 7, #2).
- Complete Jump-a-Rhyme (page 11).
- Play Operation: Rescue (page 12).
- Complete Magnetic Math (page 41).
- Continue Daily Writing Activities.
- Discuss homework: Trash or Treasure? (page 13).

Lesson III

- Discuss the friendship aspects of *Marta's Magnets*.
- Complete Attracting Friends (page 14).
- Share the "new" treasures brought in from last night's homework assignment.
- Read a friendship story (page 15).
- Play A Walk Through Town (page 48).

- Make Horseshoe Magnet Cookies (page 64).
- Continue Daily Writing Activities.

Lesson IV

- Introduce Magnetic Vocabulary (page 7, #5).
- Complete Are All Metals Magnetic? (page 16).
- Make a Magnet (page 17).
- Complete Opposites Attract (page 18).
- Conduct Boat Races (page 50).
- Make Name Magnets (page 58).
- Continue Daily Writing Activities.

Lesson V

- Review Jumprope Rhymes (page 65).
- Read the Magnetic Poems (page 32).
- Write magnet poetry (page 33).
- Perform a Balancing Act (page 19).
- Play Magnet Poles Tag (page 64).
- Visit Magnet Web Sites (page 67).
- Make Refrigerator Magnets (page 59).

Overview of Activities

Setting the Stage

1. To prepare yourself for teaching about magnets, read the following informative pages: 9, 25-26, 30, 36, 38, 53-55, 61, 67-68, and 79. Also, if you have difficulty finding a variety of magnets and magnetic items to use with your children, contact Dowling Magnets at 1-800-MAGNET-1.

2. Prepare your room by creating the bulletin board entitled Which Things Are Magnetic? (page 72).

3. Discuss the concept of collections. (An easy-reader book, *Collecting Things is Fun*!, by Kimberlee Graves, CTP, 1997, may be a helpful resource.) We collect things usually as a hobby. People collect things that bring them joy when they look at, or use, their collected items. Duplicate copies of the Collectors' Graph (page 40) for your children. Have the children circulate the room surveying their classmates to ask whether or not they collect things. A child colors the spaces in the top graph to record the number of children asked who do or do not have collections. Spaces are colored in the lower graph to record the number of boys and girls who responded that they do have collections. Discuss the results.

Enjoying the Book

1. Have your children find out what people outside the classroom like to collect. Use page 8 as a homework assignment.

2. Your children will enjoy using a daily magnetic graph. Use the bulletin board idea entitled Daily Response Graph (page 72) and set up a response board area that is sure to be a "big attraction" in your room.

3. Operation: Rescue can be set up as a learning center. Duplicate page 12 (one per child) and stack the copies in the center area. Provide the necessary materials. Review the activity's process with your children before the center is used. When a child comes to the center, he or she takes an instruction sheet, follows the directions for the activity, and records a response at the bottom of the sheet. (If you have younger children, read the directions aloud as the children do the activities. Have them give oral responses to what happened during the activity.)

4. Share ways in which your children have helped their friends or family members. Ask if any of the ways in which they have helped was accomplished by using something from a collection they have. For example, someones's baby brother or sister was crying and one of your children (the older sister or brother) gave the hurting sibling a stuffed animal to hold from his or her collection of stuffed animals.

5. Sing the Little Magnet song (page 62) and discuss why Marta might enjoy singing this song, too.

Overview of Activities *(cont.)*

Extending the Book

1. Motivate your children to search for magnets and magnetic objects at home with the Magnets at Home sheet (page 10). Allow the children to share their discoveries when they return to class with their completed sheets.

2. Read, and jump rope, to the Jumprope Rhymes (page 65). Ask the children to share any other jumprope rhymes that they know and try jumping rope to those rhymes as well.

3. Magnetic Math (page 41) has a self-checking code riddle at the bottom of the page. To solve the riddle, a child writes a letter on the answer line above its corresponding number at the bottom of the page.

4. Your children will enjoy searching for magnetic objects by completing the activity entitled That's Attractive! (page 44). Place a box filled with magnetic and nonmagnetic objects in a center area. Add a magnet fishing pole (directions, page 31). Allow the children to work individually or with a partner to complete this activity.

5. Some of the vocabulary (page 36) relating to magnets can be a bit difficult for young children. Review the definitions and encourage the children to clarify the meanings and use the words in sentences. If desired, distribute copies of page 36 to your children for future review or use. Assess the children's knowledge of these words by using Is It True? (page 37) at the end of the magnets unit.

6. Are All Metals Magnetic? is designed to guide children through a magnet activity that has been placed in a learning center. Reproduce copies of page 16 and stack them in your center area along with the necessary materials. Have the children work individually or in pairs. Each child completes page 16 by recording the activity results.

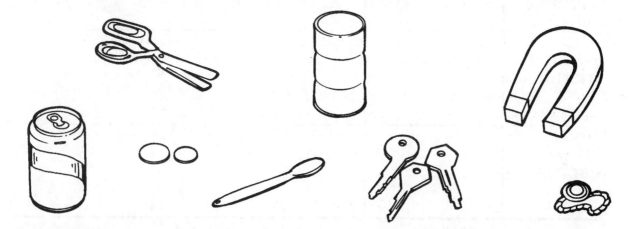

7. Page 33 contains six different forms of poetry. Introduce one poetry form and write a poem as a large group. Then encourage the children to write their own. Continue introducing the other poetry forms in the same manner (but not necessarily on the same day!). Your children's edited poems can be written and displayed using magnet pattern cutouts (page 75).

Collections

Some people collect things. Some people collect dolls, trading cards, stuffed animals, or rocks. Marta collected magnets, sticks, and cards. Do you collect things? Write about what you collect.

_____

_____

_____

Ask your friends and family what they collect. Fill in the chart below.

Person	Collection	Why They Collect Them
parent/ grandparent		
aunt/uncle		
sister/ brother		
friend		
teacher		

Why do you think people have collections?

_____

_____

Magnets At School and Home

Where are magnets or magnetic surfaces in your classroom? Have your children investigate to find out where they are in the room. Provide pairs of children with strong magnets so that they can easily determine if something is magnetic or nonmagnetic.

(**Caution:** Children should not touch magnets to computers, recorders, watches, televisions, radios, etc., as magnets can cause severe damage or ruin these items!)

After discussing the magnetic objects they have found, ask your children to think about things in their homes that are magnetic. To inspire creative thinking, explain that the inside edges of refrigerator and freezer doors have magnets in the rubber inside-door casing to help keep the door shut tight. (The children can test their refrigerator doors by holding a paper clip to the inside rubber casing or inside edges when they get home.)

Have the children brainstorm places in their homes that they think might contain magnets. Next have them brainstorm things in their homes that they think might be magnetic. List the children's responses on chart paper.

Provide copies of page 10 as a homework assignment. Explain how the chart is to be completed. (You may need to provide inexpensive refrigerator magnets for children to use who may not have magnets available to use at home.)

When the children return with their charts completed, have them share their results and ask them the following discussion questions:

–**What magnetic items did you find in your home?**

–**What did you find that was actually a magnet?**

–**Did you think something was magnetic, only to find out it wasn't?**

–**Were you surprised by any of your discoveries?**

–**What did you learn from this assignment?**

Magnets at Home

What things will attract (hold onto) your magnet? Complete the chart below.

Item	What is it made of?	Did it attract (hold) the magnet?
kitchen counter		
refrigerator		
window		
front door		
bathtub		
soup can		
plastic cup		
You pick an item:		

Look at your completed chart. What did you discover?

Jump-a-Rhyme

In the story, *Marta's Magnets*, Marta heard children chanting rhymes while jumping rope. Read one of the rhymes she heard:

One potato, two potato, three potato, four.

Jump to the window. Jump to the door.

Her new friends changed the words to make a new rhyme:

One potato, two potato, three potato, four.

A truck got stuck on Marta's door.

You can make your own jumprope rhymes, too. Complete the rhymes below by writing a second sentence that ends with the first sentence's rhyming last word.

One potato, two potato, three potato, four.

_____

Five potato, six potato, seven potato, eight.

_____

Make up a brand new jumprope rhyme. Write it on the lines below. What are the rhyming words? Share your new rhyme with a friend.

_____

_____

_____

_____

Operation: Rescue

Marta used a magnet to attract a key ring through a grate in the street. See if you can do what Marta did.

Here's what you need:

- one strong magnet
- a 3' (.9 meter) length of string
- one magnetic object (such as a nail, tack, paper clip, or key ring)

Here's what to do:

1. Toss the magnetic object behind a bookcase or under a table.
2. Tie the string tightly around the magnet.
3. Holding the free end of the string, swing the magnet toward the object. Keep trying until the magnet touches the object.

Were you able to rescue the object?

(Write yes or no.) _____

How many attempts did it take before you got the object back? _____ attempts

Write about your rescue.

_____

_____

_____

_____

_____

_____

Trash or Treasure?

Each item that Marta collected was special to her. Marta's sister just thought it was all junk. Share the old saying, *one man's trash is another man's treasure*, with the children. Discuss its meaning.

Ask the children to think about Marta's collections. Why were they special to her? What did she like about them? Why didn't her sister like her collections?

As a homework assignment, ask the children to clean out their rooms, looking for old books or toys that they no longer play with or want. (**Note:** Be certain you send home a detailed explanation to parents or guardians to explain what this homework assignment's goal is. Share with them that the children will be donating the collected items to a needy cause.)

When the children return with their items, gather the children together and allow them to share and talk about the things that they no longer want. Share with the children that they are going to get to turn their "trash" into "treasure." Share information, or better yet, have a guest speaker come in and talk to your children about the not-for-profit organization that you are going to donate the items to (such as a crisis children's or family home).

Encourage the children to write cards or letters to go along with the new treasures. If possible, have the children deliver their newly-found "treasures" to the children that will be receiving them.

This sharing-with-others activity is wonderful to do even after your magnet unit is over. During the winter holidays, or as an end-of-the-school year project, giving to others always makes one's heart feel warm and filled with love. It is important for young children to appreciate the act of giving, rather than only focusing on the act of receiving.

Dear new friend,
I hope you like your new doll. Her name is Marcy. Please love her. She loves hugs.
Your new friend,
Maggie

Here is Sammy.
Take good care of him.
Love,
Jason

Attracting Friends

Marta was able to make new friends by sharing her treasures. The children had fun learning from Marta about the way magnets work. Complete these two activities to encourage your children to make and strengthen their friendships.

Activity One

Invite your children to bring in a special toy from home. Divide the children into groups of two or three; have them take turns telling about the toys they brought in. (Each child should tell why the item is special, as well as any special instructions for how to play with the toy.) Have the small groups carefully play with one another's toys. After the playtime, gather the children in a large group for a discussion time. Ask them how it made them feel to share their valued toys. Did they enjoy watching others play with their toys? Discuss any jealous feelings that may be voiced during the discussion time (or that you observed while the children were playing). Share that we must trust our friends because that is what friendship is built on—trust.

Activity Two

Explain to your children that there are many ways to develop stronger friendships with others. Encourage the children to share their ideas for friendship-building behaviors. (You may need to share a few ideas first, such as spending time together, helping each other, or comforting a hurting friend.) Record their ideas on chart paper. Share with the children that complimenting others can foster old or new friendships (this concept may not have been one of their ideas). Ask them how they feel when someone says something nice about them. Can they remember specific compliments they were given? Model giving a compliment by asking a few children to stand next to you and giving a different verbal compliment to each of them. Ask them how being complimented made them feel. Put all of the children into pairs. Have the children exchange compliments with their partners. If the children have difficulty with this verbal sharing concept, post or share the following thought-provoking questions:

–**Is this person helpful?**
–**Is this person kind to others?**
–**Does he or she work hard in class?**
–**Does he or she share with others?**
–**Is this person artistic or creative?**
–**Does this person make people laugh?**

To encourage compliments, create a Compliment Chart by sketching a 20-square grid onto a piece of construction paper. Write the numerals 1 through 20 respectively in each square. Anytime you "catch" a child or children genuinely complimenting another child announce the good deed and add a sticker to the chart. When all twenty squares contain a sticker, the children earn a special playtime or other fun activity.

Friendship Stories

The stories detailed below have themes of sharing and friendship. After reading each story, discuss the story's main friendship theme.

The Rainbow Fish

–by Marcus Pfister (Scholastic, 1992)

Rainbow Fish was proud of his shiny scales and loved to swim past the other fish to show them off. He was unwilling to share his beautiful scales with the other fish so soon he found himself without any friends. After taking the advice of a wise octopus, Rainbow Fish decided to give each of the other fish one of his shiny scales. Sharing with the others made Rainbow Fish feel happy inside as he gained new friends.

- This touching story teaches children about the value of sharing with others.

The Giving Tree

–by Shel Silverstein (HarperCollins, 1964)

This is a beautiful story of unconditional love. Friendship between a boy and a tree endures through a lifetime as the tree gives of itself to the boy throughout all of his troubles.

- This story shows how selfishness can lead to dissatisfaction but giving to others brings happiness.

Wilfrid Gordon McDonald Partridge

–by Mem Fox (Kane/Miller Book Publishers, 1985)

This is a heart-warming story about a friendship between a young boy and an old woman. Wilfrid Gordon learns one day that his good friend, Miss Nancy, has lost her memory because she is so old. Wilfrid Gordon decides to help Miss Nancy find her memory again. He brings an assortment of precious items to Miss Nancy and as she looks at them she remembers special events in her life.

- This story will show your children that sharing memories can be a precious gift.

Friends

–by Helme Heine (Aladdin, 1986)

In this delightful story you will meet Charlie Rooster, Johnny Mouse, and Percy Pig. They wake up a barnyard, go for a morning bike ride, play hide-and-go-seek, pretend to be pirates, go fishing, munch on cherries, and pledge to be friends forever.

- This story's friendship themes are loyalty and cooperation.

Are All Metals Magnetic?

Do you think that a magnet will stick to anything that is metal? Yes or no?

Here's what you need:
- one strong magnet
- a tin can
- metal scissors
- an aluminum can
- a penny and a dime
- several metal keys
- a metal spoon and fork
- a piece of metal jewelry

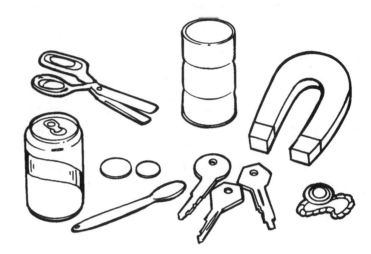

Here's what to do:

1. On the chart below, write the names of the five metal items you want to test.

2. Touch the magnet to the five items. Next to each item's name, write *yes* or *no* to tell if it was attracted (stuck) to the magnet or was not attracted to the magnet.

Object	Yes or No

Why do you think some metals are not magnetic?

_____

Make a Magnet

It's easy to make a magnet. Try it and see.

Here's what you need:
- one nail
- a strong bar magnet
- paper clips
- thumbtacks

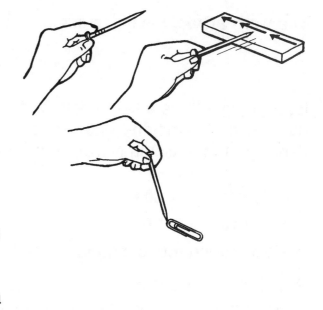

Here's what to do:
1. Hold the top end of the nail between your fingers.

2. Rub the pointed end of the nail across the magnet. Stroke the magnet *in the same direction* 30 to 40 times. (Remember, do not stroke the nail in a back-and-forth motion!)

3. Now try to pick up a paper clip or a thumbtack with the nail. What happened?

_____

_____

Now try this:
1. Hold the nail about six inches (15 cm) above a table and drop the nail.

2. Pick up the nail and try to attract (hold) a paper clip with the nail. What happened? Why?

_____

_____

_____

Opposites Attract

The word *repel* means to push away.

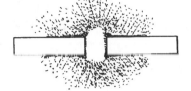

The word *attract* means to come together.

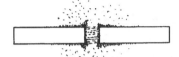

Every magnet has a North pole and a South pole. Poles that are the same (North-North or South-South) *repel* each other. Poles that are opposites (North-South or South-North) *attract* each other.

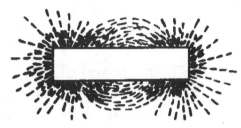

Here's what you need:
- two strong bar magnets
- two strong round magnets

Here's what you do:
1. Put the ends of the two bar magnets together. Did the ends repel or attract? Now turn one of the bar magnets around and put the ends together again. Did something different happen? Why?

   _____

   _____

2. Try putting two round magnets together. First try to put the magnets together top-to-bottom. Did the magnets repel or attract each other? Turn one of the magnets over and put the magnets together again. What happened this time?

   _____

   _____

3. Now try to put the round magnets together side-to-side. Did the magnets repel or attract each other?

   _____

   _____

18

Balancing Act

When you try to put two like poles together (North-North or South-South), you can feel the magnetic force (power) pushing between the two poles. Just how strong is this force?

Here's what you need:

- a pencil
- four or five strong ring magnets
- a ruler

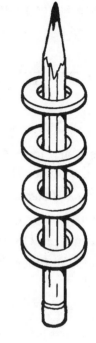

Here's what to do:

1. Hold the pencil vertically with the eraser end resting on a flat surface.

2. One at a time, slide the ring magnets onto the pencil. If any magnet sticks tightly to another magnet, remove it, turn it over, and place it back onto the pencil.

3. Using the ruler, measure the distance between each of the magnets.

What was the distance between each magnet? _____

Write about why you think the magnets did not stick together while on the pencil.

_____

_____

_____

Why do you think there was space between each magnet?

_____

_____

_____

What Makes a Magnet?

by Franklyn M. Branley

Summary

What Makes a Magnet? *explains how magnets work. This informative book discusses magnet poles, the earth as a giant magnet, how magnets can be made, how to make a compass, and much, much more!*

Sample Plan

Lesson I

- Explore Marvelous Magnets (page 21, Setting the Stage, #1).
- Read *What Makes a Magnet?*
- Complete What is a Magnet? (page 25).
- Try to Line 'em Up! (page 26).
- Make a Giant Floor Venn Diagram (page 42).
- Select a Daily Writing Activity (pages 34 and 35).

Lesson II

- Reread or review *What Makes a Magnet?* focusing on the compass information.
- Make a Compass (page 21, #3).
- Sing The Compass song (page 62).
- Play It's Compass Time! (page 66).
- Continue Daily Writing Activities.

Lesson III

- Sing all of the magnet songs (page 62).
- Write a song about magnets (page 63).
- Learn about Magnetic Fields (page 28).
- Investigate Iron Filings (page 29).
- Make a Funny Face (page 21, #4).
- Learn about, and write, a magnet legend (page 38).

Lesson IV

- Learn about William Gilbert and Michael Faraday (pages 54 and 55).
- Begin researching scientists (page 23, #4).
- Complete Earth: A Giant Magnet (page 30).
- Make Magnetic Earth Art (page 61).
- Begin discussing and developing the Magnetic Talk Show (page 70).

Lesson V

- Make and test scientific predictions (page 22, #2).
- Plan and conduct Scientific Method experiments (page 52).
- Learn about Magnets in Everyday Life (page 53).
- Complete Hang On! (page 46).
- Continue preparing for the Magnetic Talk Show.

Lesson VI

- Assess gained knowledge via Is It True? (page 37).
- Fish for Magnet Facts (page 31).
- Conduct a dress rehearsal for the Magnetic Talk Show.
- Begin A Magnetic Experience (page 69).

Overview of Activities

Setting the Stage

1. Before engaging in structured magnet experiments, allow the children to explore magnets on their own. Arrange a center area in your room, complete with different shapes and sizes of magnets and magnetic materials. (See the Bibliography, page 79, if you have difficulty finding magnets in your area.) Duplicate copies of page 24 for the children to complete as they explore.

2. Have your children create a Giant Floor Venn Diagram (page 42) to discover objects in the classroom that are, or have parts that are, magnetic, nonmagnetic, or both.

Enjoying the Book

1. Create a science exploration center to allow your children to conduct or reconduct some magnet experiments. Provide duplicated copies of pages 24–25 and pages 27–30, as well as any necessary science materials. The children can write their thoughts and findings in a science journal (page 35). When they finish an experiment, they can fill out a journal sheet and add it to their personal portfolios or keep them in science journal binders.

2. The book *What Makes a Magnet?* shows children an illustration of how the iron particles in a needle can be aligned in order to make it magnetic. Show your children how this happens by demonstrating Line 'em Up! (page 26). If desired, after demonstrating the experimental process, place this activity in your science exploration center to allow the children to try it on their own.

3. Make a Compass can be done as a class project in small cooperative groups or as an activity in your science exploration center. For science center use, duplicate one copy of page 27. Affix the copy to a sheet of tagboard; laminate it for durability. Place the directional sheet in the science center along with the necessary materials. Go over the procedure with your children and then let them complete the experment on their own. (*Optional:* The children may want to try to make the compass that is described and illustrated in *What Makes a Magnet?* If so, provide the necessary materials at the science center so that your children can try the book's compass design, as well.

4. Make a Funny Face is an activity similar to the one described in *What Makes a Magnet?* Duplicate page 60 and glue it to a piece of sturdy cardboard (one face for every two children). Provide the pairs of children with iron filings (see Bibliography, Magnet Resources, page 79) and a strong bar magnet. As one child holds the cardboard flat horizontally, the partner places some iron filings on top of the cardboard and moves the bar magnet underneath the cardboard to make a mustache and beard, as well as fill in the eyebrows and the hair on the face using the iron filings.

5. If you have not already done so, make a batch of Horseshoe Magnet Cookies (page 64) for the children to munch on.

Overview of Activities *(cont.)*

Extending the Book

1. The Write a Song activity (page 63) can be used as an individual assignment or be completed as a group activity. For completing as a group activity, copy the song outlines onto chart paper. Encourage the children to suggest appropriate words to complete each song.

2. Before asking the children to create and conduct their own original magnet experiments, demonstrate a simple experiment. Begin by copying The Scientific Method (page 52) onto chart paper and discussing each part of the method. Share the concept via a verbalized experiment. Here is one example:

Question

Will a magnet attract—hold—a paper clip through a wooden door?

Prediction

I think that the magnet will attract—hold—the paper clip through the door.

Steps

1. I hold the magnet to one side of the door.
2. I hold the paper clip to the other side of the door in the same area as where I am holding the magnet on the other side of the door.
3. I let go of the paper clip.

Result

The paper clip fell. The magnet did not attract—hold—the paper clip.

Conclusion

I think the door is too thick and the magnet isn't strong enough to force the paper clip to stay attached to the door.

Overview of Activities *(cont.)*

Extending the Book *(cont.)*

Many children have difficulty making predictions for fear of failure. You may want to complete page 51, I Predict..., as a large group before having the children create their own original magnet experiments.

When you are ready for them to create original experiments, provide the children with copies of page 52 and allow them to conduct their outlined magnet experiments.

3. As the children learn about William Gilbert (page 54) and Michael Faraday (page 55), mention the culminating activity, a Magnet Talk Show (page 69). Explain to the students that two children will assume the roles of the two scientists, while the rest of the children will also have special roles in the Magnet Talk Show production.

4. Have your children learn about other scientists. The Scientist Research sheet (page 57) will provide your children with questions to answer while conducting their research. Possible scientists (not all are magnet-focused) might be:

Hans Oersted	**Alexander Graham Bell**
Andre Ampere	**Thomas Edison**
Charles Coulomb	**George Washington Carver**
Joseph Henry	**Eli Whitney**

Provide resource books, encyclopedias, and computer encyclopedia programs, if available, to help in the researching process. If your children are Internet-accessible, they may want to try some of the Web sites listed on page 67 or conduct a Web search (page 68). Display the completed research reports on the bulletin board entitled Great Minds...(page 73).

5. The earth is actually a huge magnet. The center of the earth, the inner core, is made of iron and nickel. When the inner core moves and rubs against the outer core, it makes a magnetic field. Use page 30 to help your children understand the earth's magnetic pull and then share these amazing animal earth facts:

–Compass Termites in Australia always build their nests facing North.

–Whales and dolphins have a built-in, natural magnet that uses the Earth's magnetic field to help them navigate.

Marvelous Magnets

Explore what magnets can do. Write a sentence about what happened when you used each kind of magnet. What kinds of things did the magnets attract (hold)?

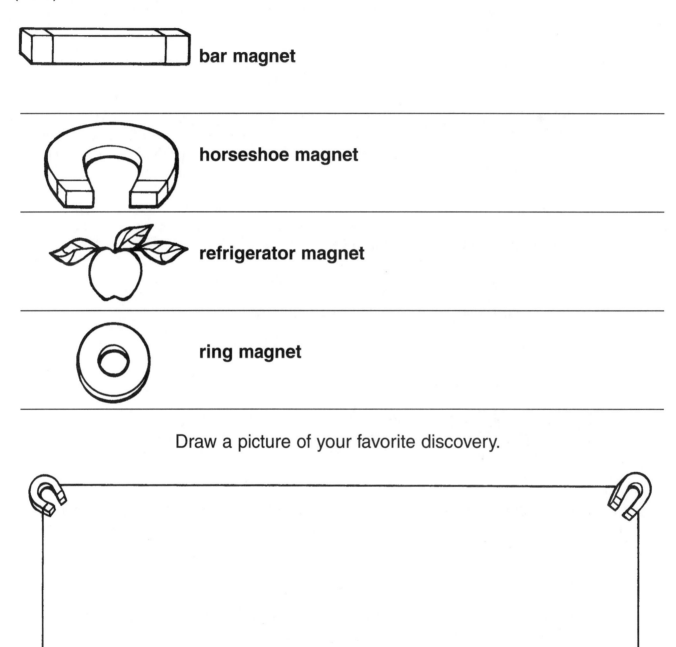

bar magnet

_____

horseshoe magnet

_____

refrigerator magnet

_____

ring magnet

_____

Draw a picture of your favorite discovery.

What is a Magnet?

A natural magnet is a certain kind of rock. Sometimes this rock is called magnetite or a lodestone. Magnetite is found in or on the ground.

Magnets can also be manmade. They are made of steel. Steel has iron in it. Manmade magnets are made in all kinds of shapes and sizes.

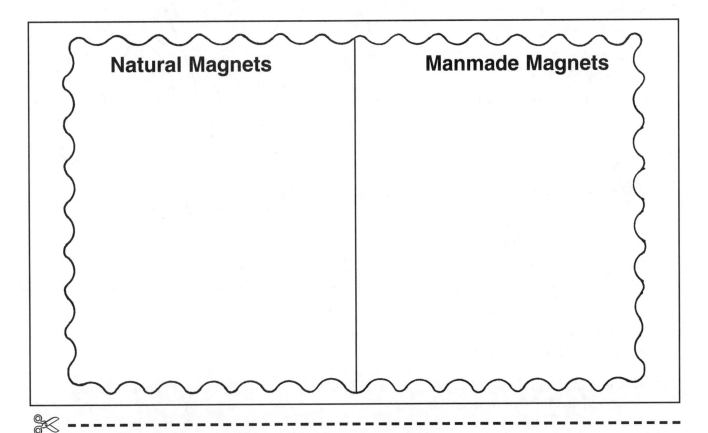

Natural Magnets   **Manmade Magnets**

Cut and paste the natural and manmade magnets.

Line 'em Up!

What happens to a nail that makes it magnetic after being stroked with a magnet (page 17)? Scientists aren't exactly sure, but here's what they think. A nail is made of tiny particles of iron. These particles are scattered in different directions within the object. By stroking it with a magnet, the iron particles line up in a straight fashion (polarize) and a magnetic force is produced. Try this activity with your children to demonstrate particles polarizing.

Materials

- a small, clear vial
- some iron filings
- a magnifying lens
- a strong horseshoe magnet
- a compass

Directions

1. Fill the small vial with iron filings.

2. Use the magnifying lens to look closely at the arrangement of the filings in the vial. Is there a pattern or do the filings look randomly scattered?

3. Using only one pole (end) of the horseshoe magnet, stroke the vial 30 to 40 times *in the same direction*. Try to hold the vial as still as possible while stroking it with the magnet.

4. Now use the magnifying lens again. What do you notice? (The iron filings should be more organized and lined up with one another.)

5. Continue to keep the vial steady and place it near a compass. What happens? (The magnetic force within the vial should be able to influence the direction of the compass needle.)

6. Shake the vial to mix up the iron filings. Now test the magnetic pull of the vial with the compass. Is the magnetic pull still present? Try using the compass again after you stroke the vial of filings a second time (30 to 40 times *in the same direction*.) What happened this time?

Make a Compass

If a magnet is able to float or hang freely, it will act like a compass and point to the north.

Here's what you need:

- a nail

- a strong bar magnet

- a piece of Styrofoam (a bit larger than the nail)

- masking tape

- a small bowl of water

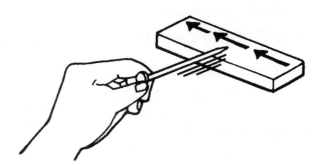

Here's what to do:

1. Turn your nail into a magnet. Stroke the nail on the magnet 30 to 40 times *in the same direction.*

2. Tape the nail to the piece of Styrofoam. Gently float the Styrofoam on top of the water with the nail facing up. Be sure there are no other magnetic objects near by.

3. Wait until the floating nail stops moving. Is the nail pointing North? Use the compass to check to see if the nail is pointing North.

4. Try the experiment again. Follow step 1 again first. This time when you put the Styrofoam and nail on the water's surface, spin the nail. Wait for it to stop moving. Did the nail point north this time, too? Check the nail's direction by using the compass.

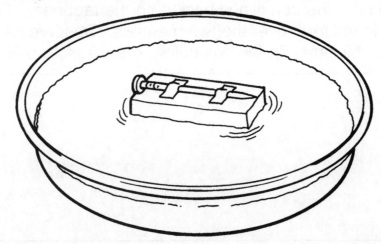

Magnetic Fields

When you try to touch two like poles together (north-north or south-south), you can feel the force (resistance) of the magnetic field between them. This experiment will let you see what that force looks like.

Here's what you need:

- two strong bar magnets

- one 9" x 6" (22½ cm x 15½ cm) strip of tagboard

- some iron filings

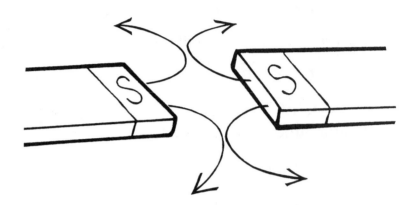

Here's what to do:

1. Place the bar magnets on a tabletop. They should be 2" (5 cm) apart. Set the tagboard on top of the magnets.

2. Sprinkle some iron filings onto the tagboard. Observe what happens to the filings. In the box below, draw a picture of what happened.

```



```

3. Remove the iron filings and wipe off the tagboard. Move the two magnets one more inch (2.54 cm) apart. Put the tagboard strip back down on the magnets and pour the iron filings back onto the tagboard. Gently slide the tagboard back and forth over the two magnets. Observe what happens to the iron filings this time. In the box below, draw a picture of what happened.

```



```

Iron Filings

Iron filings are in the salt! Can you get them out?

Here's what you need:

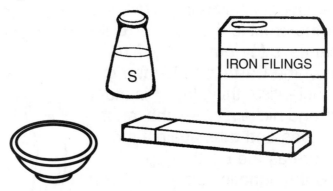

- a small bowl of salt
- a small bowl of iron filings
- a craft stick
- a small sheet of tagboard
- two small stacks of books
- a strong bar magnet

Here's what you do:

1. Pour the iron filings into the bowl of salt. Mix up the salt and the iron filings with the craft stick.

2. Pour the mixture onto the piece of tagboard.

3. Suspend the tagboard between two stacks of books.

4. Move the magnet back and forth *under* the tagboard. Can you attract the iron filings with the magnet and move them away from the salt?

Write about what you did.	**Draw a picture of what you did.**

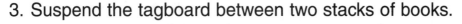
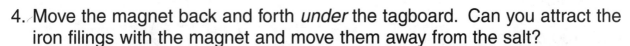
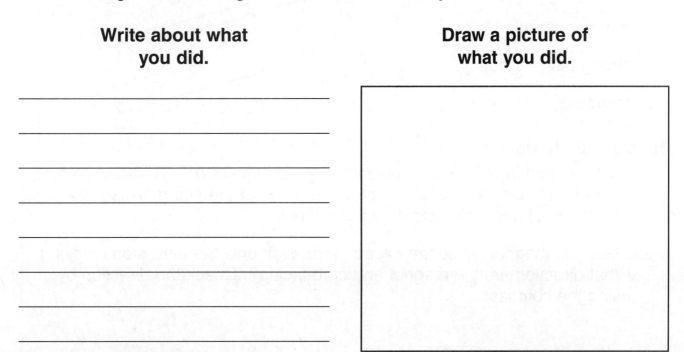

Earth: A Giant Magnet

The Earth has different layers. The outside layer is called the *crust.* Under the crust is the *mantle.* Below the mantle is the *outer core.* The center of the Earth is called the *inner core.* Scientists think that it is made of iron and nickel. When the inner core moves and rubs against the outer core as the Earth is spinning, it creates a magnetic field. The Earth acts like a big magnet. It has a north pole (top of the Earth) and a south pole (bottom of the Earth). The Earth's natural magnetic pull forces a magnet to line up in a north–south direction.

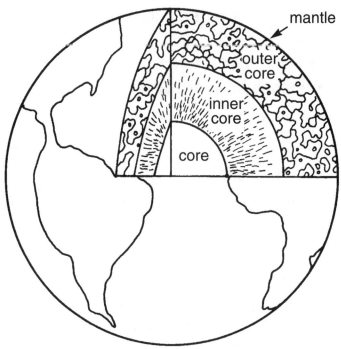

Here's what you need:

- 3" x 5" (8 cm x 13 cm) index card

- hole punch

- 12" (30 cm) length of string

- ornament hook

- strong bar magnet

- compass

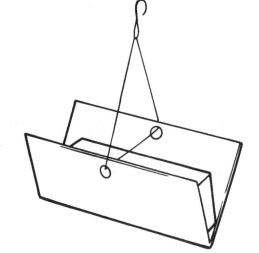

Here's what to do:

1. Fold the card in half. Punch holes in the card as shown. Thread the string through the holes and tie the hook to the ends of the string. Attach the hook to a chalkrail or simply hold it with your fingers.

2. Place the magnet inside the folded card. Wait until the card stops moving. What direction are the magnet and card facing? Check the direction by using the compass.

Fish for Magnet Facts

Fishing Pole

Make a magnetic fishing pole by attaching a two-foot (61 cm) length of yarn to the end of a yard or meter stick. Tie a strong magnet to the end of the string.

Fish

From construction paper, cut out twenty fish shapes. Write one of the true facts below on each of ten fish, as well as making up ten untrue facts to write on the remaining ten fish. Attach a small strip of self-sticking magnetic tape to the tail of each fish cutout. If magnetic tape is not available, you can use large paper clips clipped to the tails. Place the prepared fish in an empty children's wading pool or in a box covered with blue construction paper.

To Play

Have your children take turns using the fishing pole to fish for the magnet facts. As each child retrieves a fact, have him or her read the fact aloud or hand it to you to be read aloud. Allow the children to respond to the facts (true or false), state their reasoning, and ask any questions that may help them to clarify their learning.

Ten True Magnet Facts

1. **Some rocks are magnetic.**

2. **A magnet has a north pole and a south pole.**

3. **On two magnets, the opposite poles will attract.**

4. **Magnets are attracted to iron.**

5. **The Earth is a giant natural magnet.**

6. **A compass is a small magnet.**

7. **The Earth has a north pole and a south pole.**

8. **A compass points north because of the earth's magnetic pull.**

9. **Magnetic force makes the end of two magnets push away or pull together.**

10. **Michael Faraday and William Gilbert are famous magnet scientists.**

Magnet Poems

Magnets Everywhere

Magnets are here, magnets are there,
We can see magnets most anywhere!
We find them in shower curtains, and
even in cabinets,
Everywhere we look we see wonderful magnets!
They stick to soda cans, needles, and nails,
The strength of magnets just never fails.
Magnets are here, magnets are there,
We can see magnets most anywhere!

Cinquain Poem

magnet
smooth, metal
attracting, collecting, holding
makes our lives easier
horseshoe

Acrostic Poem

Magnetic
Attracts things
Good for holding papers
North and south poles
Every refrigerator needs one
They are terrific!

Riddle Poem

I am hard. I am shaped like a U.
I am very "attractive." What am I?

(*Answer: a horseshoe magnet*)

Alliterative Poem

They are magical, marvelous, and a-mazingly mysterious,
Those miraculous, magnificent, magnetic magnets!

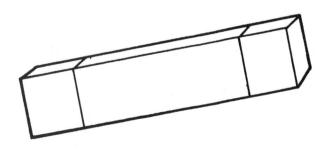

By Numbers Poem

Magnet
North pole
South pole, too
Picks up iron things
Magnets can be handy tools

Magnetic Poetry Ideas

Samples of each of these poetry styles can be found on page 32. After children write their original magnet poems, have them copy edited versions onto duplicated horseshoe magnet patterns (page 75) and display their poetic talents.

Rhyming Verse

A poem wherein every two line's last words rhyme.

Cinquain

Line 1—Title (one noun)

Line 2—Description of title (two adjectives)

Line 3—An action about the title (three verbs)

Line 4—A feeling about the title (a four-word phrase)

Line 5—Another word for the title (one-word synonym)

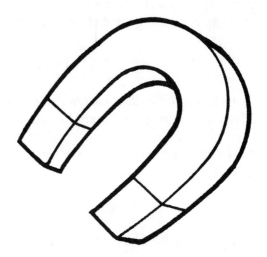

Acrostic

Choose a word and write it vertically. For each letter of the word, write a word or phrase that is related to the original word.

Riddle Poem

Give clues about a chosen object, person, or animal. The reader has to guess what the riddle is describing.

Alliterative Poem

Alliteration occurs by when a specific beginning consonant sound is repeated throughout the poem in as many words of the poem as possible.

By Numbers Poem

Line 1—one word

Line 2—two words

Line 3—three words

Line 4—four words

Line 5—five words

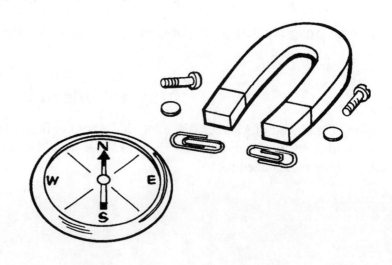

Daily Writing Activities

If I Were a Magnet

Remind the children that magnets attract things containing iron. Have them imagine that they could attract anything they want to (such as pizza, chocolate, toys, etc.). Have the children write stories, and illustrate them, describing what they would attract and how they would use their special abilities.

Would You Rather?

Read, or post, one of the thought questions below and have your children respond pictorially and in writing. Be certain to remind them to state their reasoning.

–*What you rather discover something new about magnets or invent something using magnets?*

–*Would you rather have a rock collection or a magnet collection?*

–*Would you rather have a television or a computer?*

–*Would you rather have a bar magnet, a ring magnet, or a horseshoe magnet?*

Writing Couplets

A couplet consists of two lines of poetry. Each line has the same number of beats and the ending words rhyme. Here are two examples:

Magnets repel and they attract,
This is a known "matter" of fact.

Compass, compass, you're my friend,
Help me find my way again.

Make up some group couplets with your children and then have them try to write some couplets on their own.

Magnes' Dilemma

After sharing the legend of Magnes (page 38), have your children write about what they would do if they were in Magnes' predicament. Ask them to share what they would have done once they were released from the magnetized rock.

Daily Writing Activities *(cont.)*

A World Without Electromagnets

We use electromagnets for so many things in our everyday life (page 53 and 55). What would life be like without them? Have children write about how their lives would be different without computers, television, lamps, telephones, or cars. What would they do for light in their homes? How would they contact their friends? How would they get around town? What would they do for fun?

If I Were a Scientist

Scientists have invented most of the technology used in our homes and schools. Some scientists have invented ways to help sick people get better. Other scientists have invented things that make our lives easier. Ask the children to write about and illustrate something they would like to invent and how it would help society. First they will need to think of a problem that needs to be solved and then they will need to come up with the solution (the invention). Allow them time to brainstorm ideas, write out their design concepts, rewrite and illustrate their designs, and if possible, actually create their inventions.

Questions, Questions

Your children may have on-going questions about magnets and how they work. Encourage them to write a list of questions. Have the children share their questions with you and their classmates and determine how they might go about finding the answers. For those that may not have any questions, ask them to write about some of the information they have learned throughout the unit.

Science Journals

Duplicate several copies of the journal sheet (page 77) for each child. Staple the sheets together or place them in a three hole-punch folder.

The journal sheet are designed to encourage your children to reflect on newly gained knowledge, ask questions, and draw pictures to illustrate their "magnetic" experiences.

Unit Management

Science Journal

I've learned that...

I've been wondering about...

Here's a picture of something I did.

© *Teacher Created Materials, Inc.*   77   #2377 *Thematic Unit—Magnets*

Magnetic Vocabulary

magnet–a piece of iron or steel that attracts certain metals

attract–to pull close

repel–to push away

magnetic pole–the strongest point on a magnet

magnetic object–something that is attracted to a magnet

force–energy that can cause something to be pushed or pulled

demagnetize–to take away the magnetic ability of a magnet

compass–an instrument with a needle that points North and is used to determine directions

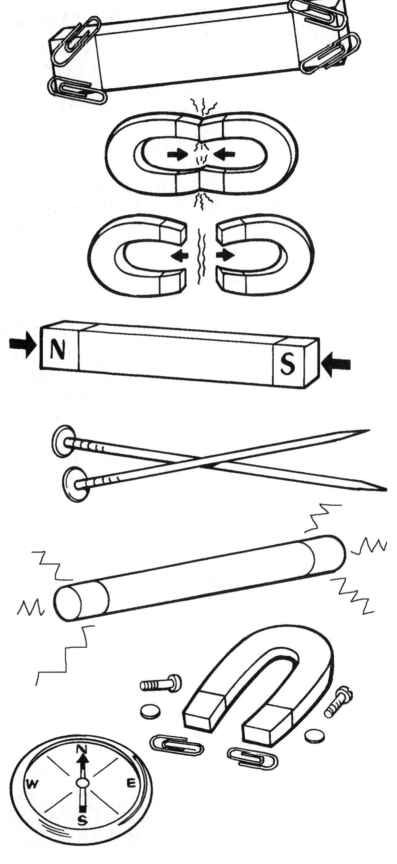

Is it True?

Read each statement below. Write *true* or *false* on the line in front of each statement. If the statement is false, write a new sentence below it to make the statement true.

1. Something that is attracted to a magnet is a **magnetic object.**

_____

_____

2. A **compass** is the strongest point on a magnet.

_____

_____

3. To take away a magnet's force is to **demagnetize** it.

_____

_____

4. A **magnetic pole** is a metal bar.

_____

_____

5. To **repel** means to push away.

_____

_____

6. When two magnets **attract,** they do not stick together.

_____

_____

7. **Force** causes an object to push or pull.

_____

_____

Legends

A legend is a story about an event that happened a long time ago. Usually a legend has some truth to it, but untruths have often been added through the years. There is a Greek legend about how magnets were first discovered.

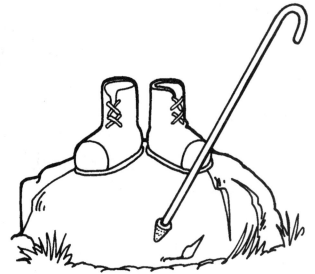

Thousands of years ago an old man named Magnes was herding his sheep. As he walked his sheep through the fields, he climbed on a large, black rock to get a better view. Something strange happened. The nails in his shoes and the metal at the tip of his shepherd's staff stuck to the rock! He lifted his feet out of his shoes and left his staff to go tell the townspeople of Magnesia what happened. They came to look at the mysterious rock. The townspeople were amazed. Magnes then removed his shoes and staff and went on his way. The townspeople named the black rock "magnetite" after the old man and the town nearby.

Over the years, legends were made up about the power of magnetite. Some legends told of magnetite having magical powers. Others told of magnetite healing the sick and driving evil spirits away. Sailors told legends of ships made of iron being attracted to magnetite rocks only to be crushed and shipwrecked.

Activities

1. Explain to your children what legends are and how they often change over time. Tell your children the legend of how magnetite was discovered (italics story above). Then have your children create a Big Book (page 39) sequencing the story that you shared with them.

2. Write group or individual legends. Have the children decide on something they would like to explain in legend form. Here are a few suggestions:

> **–Why the sun is yellow**
>
> **–How the moon got in the sky**
>
> **–Why a zebra has stripes**
>
> **–How the giraffe got its long neck**
>
> **–Why grasshoppers hop**
>
> **–How the oceans got waves**

Making a Big Book

Big books are a wonderful, language arts experience that combines reading, writing, speaking, listening, and encourages artistic creativity.

Steps

1. Before making the big books, gather all of the children into one group and review the information studied and facts they have learned. Brainstorm or review a list of vocabulary words that might be useful when writing the big books (page 36).

2. Provide each child or cooperative group (group size should not exceed four children) with five large sheets of paper (at least 12" x 18" [30cm x 46cm]). One sheet will serve as the book's cover. The children may want to write a title on the cover first or choose to wait until the remainder of the book is completed.

3. On each of the remaining four sheets (pages), the children write the story. The story's text should be written at the bottom of each page and an illustration drawn above the written information.

   If desired, for younger children, have them dictate their desired text to an adult who in turn writes the shared information on each page.

4. Have the children or an adult stack the completed pages in correct sequence (title page followed by the information pages), align the edges, and staple the pages together along the left edge to create the book's spine.

5. Encourage the children to read their stories to one another. If desired, have the children share their stories with other children during library time or by visiting other classrooms.

Collectors' Graph

Do your classmates collect things? Ask them. For each person you ask, color in a yes or no space.

Yes												
		1	2	3	4	5	6	7	8	9	10	11	12
No												

Do more boys or girls have collections? Color a space for each boy or girl who said they have a collection.

Girls												
		1	2	3	4	5	6	7	8	9	10	11	12
Boys												

What did you discover? _____

40

Magnetic Math

Solve the problems. Match the answer letters to the numbers at the bottom of the sheet to solve the riddle.

---

1. John's magnet held 3 paper clips.
   Sarah's magnets held 7 paper clips.
   How many more paper clips does Sarah's magnet hold? _____ **N**

---

2. Chang used his magnet to pick up 2 keys,
   1 paper clip, and 4 pins.
   How many items were picked up altogether? _____ **T**

---

3. Ashley had 9 magnets.
   She gave 2 magnets to Jodi.
   She gave 1 magnet to Seth.
   How many magnets does Ashley still have? _____ **A**

---

4. David has 12 magnets.
   Tomeka has 7 magnets.
   How many more magnets does David have? _____ **M**

---

5. A ring magnet attracted 9 pins.
   A bar magnet attracted 8 pins.
   How many pins were attracted altogether? _____ **G**

---

6. Jesse found alot of magnets at home.
   He found 3 refrigerator magnets,
   1 can opener magnet, and
   5 shower magnets.
   How many magnets did he find in all? _____ **E**

What kind of net sticks to a refrigerator?

A ___ ___ ___ ___ ___ ___
    5   6   17   4   9   7

Giant Floor Venn Diagram

Some objects are magnetic, other objects are not magnetic. Some objects have parts that are magnetic and parts that are not. For example, show your children a pencil. Ask the children if they think the pencil is magnetic or not magnetic. Encourage them to look at the different parts of the pencil—the wood, graphite, eraser, and the metal around the eraser. Test the different parts of the pencil with a strong magnet. Ask them what they discovered. Conduct the same demonstration with a desk, a chair, and a few other classroom items. Draw and label a Venn diagram similar to the one below on the chalkboard or chart paper. Explain how to complete the diagram. Record what was learned about the pencil.

Magnetic   **Nonmagnetic**

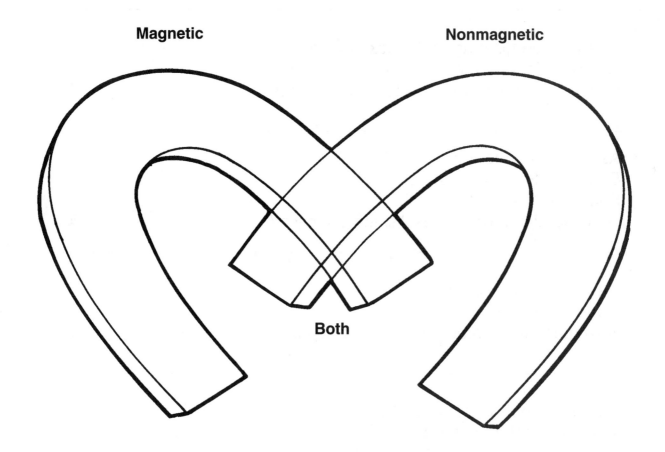

Both

Explain how a Venn diagram can be especially fun to do when it is created on the floor. Move the desks and other appropriate furniture to the sides of the room. Using two long lengths of yarn, make two large, overlapping horseshoe-shaped magnets on the floor. Label each section of the horseshoe-magnet Venn diagram using three sheets of paper: *magnetic, nonmagnetic*, and *both*. Place the labels above and below the appropriate areas and let the fun begin! Invite the children to "magnetically" explore actual items in the room and place the items in the correct diagram areas on the floor. For example, magnetic containers and paper clips would be placed in the section labeled *magnetic*. Items such as glue bottles and crayons would be place in the section labeled *nonmagnetic*. Items such as a chair or pencil may be placed in the section labeled *both* if appropriate.

When the activity is completed, have the children draw their own Venn diagrams on paper and illustrate and label the items placed on the actual floor diagram.

Magnetic Attractions

To complete this activity, every two to three children will need a magnetic wand (Magnet Resources, Bibliography, page 79) and a very large handful of jumbo paper clips.

Explain the mathematical procedure to your children. Tell them that they will be practicing counting by sets of five using tally marks. (The fun is that the tally marks will be the paper clips themselves.) Have each group place their pile of paper clips on a tabletop or other flat surface area. Each child in the group takes a turn using a magnetic wand to make a "sweep" through the paper clips (by dragging the wand through the pile). Whatever paper clips remain attached to the wand are then placed in a separate smaller pile. After each child in the group makes his or her sweep, the group proceeds to the next step, tallying the final count. Show the children how to count the paper clips in a tally-mark fashion (see illustration below). They will need to vertically line up four paper clips side-by-side, then take a fifth paper clip and place it directly on top of the four paper clips in a diagonal fashion so that the paper clips look like a set of five tallies.

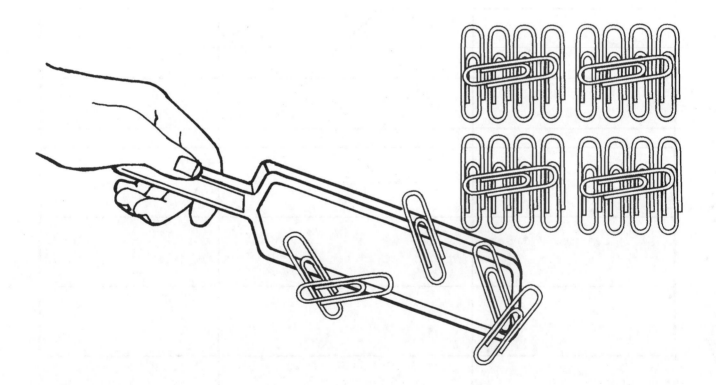

The children then make sets of five tally marks until they have used all of their paper clips from their two-to-three sweep total. Have all of the groups share their results. If mathematically appropriate, have the children figure out the average total of swept paper clips by combining the group totals and dividing that total by the number of small groups.

You can also create a subtraction extension by giving the children a predetermined number of paper clips, having them make a predetermined number of sweeps through the pile, and subtracting the total swept from the original pile's total number of paper clips.

Science

That's Attractive!

Look through the box of objects. What objects would a magnet attract? On the chart below, list eight objects. For each object, answer the first question. Use the fishing pole to try to pick up the object and answer the second question.

Objects	Will it be attracted to the magnet? (yes or no)	Was it attracted? (yes or no)

Did any of your discoveries surprise you? Why or why not?

_____

_____

Can You Make Magnets?

A nail can become a magnet. What else can become a magnet? Look at the objects listed below. Make your predictions. Stroke each object 30 to 40 times on the magnet *in the same direction* to see if it turns into a magnet (hold a paper clip to each item to test it).

Item	What do you predict? (Write yes or no.)	Did it become a magnet? (Write yes or no.)
eraser		
twig		
penny		
nickel		
rock		
cardboard		
scissors		

On the back of this paper, draw a picture of the objects that became magnetic.

Hang On!

Some magnets are stronger than others. Try testing the strength of magnets by seeing how many paper clips you can hang from one magnet.

Here's what you need:
- different sizes and shapes of magnets

- paper clips

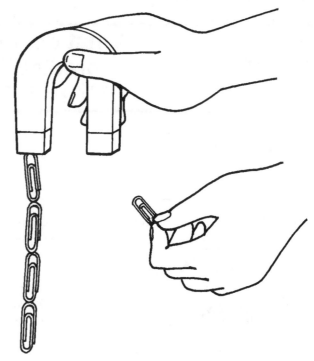

Here's what to do:
1. Choose one of the magnets and attach a paper clip to it.

2. Try to attach another paper clip to the first paper clip by touching the second paper clip to the first paper clip.

3. Continue to add paper clips until the paper clips you are adding do not hold on to each other. How many total paper clips are hanging from the magnet?_____ paper clips

4. Try to make chains of paper clips using some of the other magnets. Now answer these questions:

   Which magnet was the strongest? _____

   How many paper clips did it hold? _____

   Which magnet was the weakest?_____

   How many paper clips did it hold? _____

On the back of this paper, draw a picture of the strongest magnet and how many paper clips it held.

Water Rescue

Materials

- empty, clear 2-liter plastic bottle (cut away the top portion)
- water
- copies of the pictures below (colored, cutout, and laminated)
- self-sticking magnetic tape
- a small amount of modeling clay
- a 16" (41 cm) length of string
- a strong ring or bar magnet

Directions

1. Place pieces of magnetic tape on the backs of the following prepared pictures: key, ring, coins, diver, license plate, and soda can. Attach a small piece of clay to the remaining objects (to weigh them down).

2. Fill the 2-liter bottle two-thirds full with water. Drop all of the prepared pictures into the water.

3. Attach the magnet to one end of the string. Have the children decide which objects need rescuing. Allow them to retrieve them from the water using the strung magnet.

4. Ask the children to share what their retrieved objects have in common and what the remaining objects have in common. Ask the children to share why they retrieved the items they chose to rescued by stating their reasoning.

Magnet Races

A Walk Through Town

Preparing the Gameboard

Duplicate the gameboard (page 49) onto cardstock, color it, and laminate it for durability.

Preparing the Magnet Sticks

Attach strong magnets to one end of two rulers by tying them on with a string or hot gluing into place.

Preparing the Game Pieces

Duplicate, color, cut out, and laminate the girl and boy game pieces (patterns at right). To prepare the game pieces; fold Line 1 *away* from the printed pattern; crease. Fold Line 2 *down and back*, toward the front of the printed pattern; glue the "flapped" section together; allow to dry. Attach a piece of self-sticking magnetic tape to the bottom of each game piece.

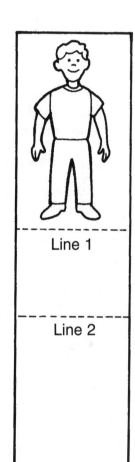

Line 1

Line 2

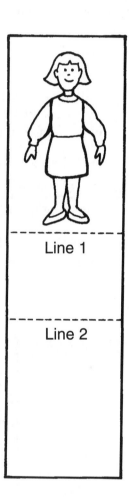

Line 1

Line 2

Playing the Game

Suspend the gameboard between two stacks of books. Two players can compete at one time. Each player places his or her game piece on one of the two houses. To navigate the magnetic game pieces, the children place their magnet sticks *under* the gameboard, directly beneath their individual game pieces. The object of the game is to move the game piece through the path to the opposite house without touching the sides of the path along the way. A third child may act as referee, determining if the sides were touched and who reached the park first.

A Walk Through Town

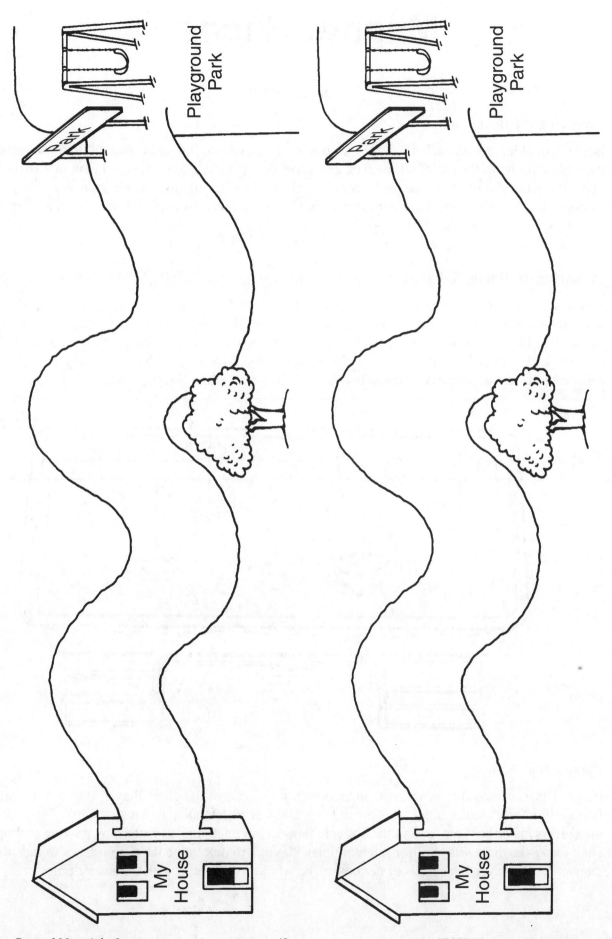

Magnet Races *(cont.)*

Boat Races

Preparing the Boat Course

Begin by making the obstacle flags for the course. To make one flag, glue a small, red, triangular, paper flag cutout to the top of a toothpick and stand the opposite end of the toothpick in a small ball of clay. Press the ball of clay onto the bottom of a clear, glass baking dish. Make as many obstacle flags as desired and add to dish. Fill the baking dish with one inch (2.54 cm) of water. Set the filled dish on two stacks of books so that there is a fair amount of space beneath the dish for moving a magnet stick (see directions for making a magnet stick, page 48).

Preparing the Racing Boats

To make a racing boat, cut out one "cup" from a Styrofoam® egg carton. Trim the edges of the cup to make them even. Press a small ball of clay into the inside bottom of the cup. Cut out a small, blue, square flag from construction paper and glue it to a toothpick; stand the toothpick flag in the ball of clay. Attach a square of self-sticking magnetic tape to the underside of the cup. Make a second boat following the same assembly process, but this time make a yellow-flagged boat.

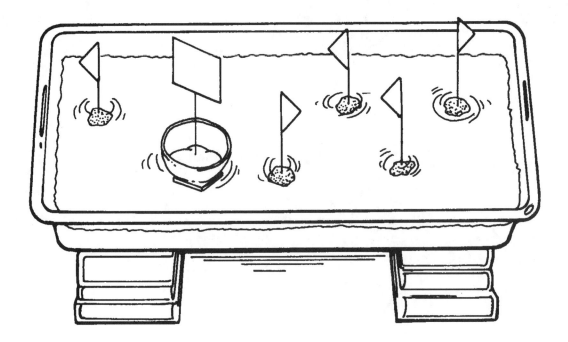

Playing the Game

Player 1 places his or her racing boat in the water at one end of the dish. Player 2 (or a third child who is playing referee) looks at the second-hand of a clock or watch and announces, "Go!" Player 1 maneuvers his or her boat around the obstacle flags in a predetermined pattern by moving the magnet stick *under* the dish. Player 2 (or referee) times Player 1 to determine the time it takes to race the course. Then Player 2 races his or her boat. The winner is the child with the fastest time.

I Predict...

A prediction is something that you think will happen.

Scientists make predictions about experiments. Sometimes scientists are right and sometimes they are not, that is part of making predictions and being a scientist.

Read the two experiments below. Write your prediction on the lines and then try the experiments.

1. Place a paper clip in a clear, plastic cup filled with water. Touch a magnet to the outside of the cup. Do you think you can make the paper clip move?

Prediction: _____

_____

Try it. What happened? _____

_____

_____

2. Rub the end of a toothpick across a bar magnet. Stroke it 30 times *in the same direction*. Touch the toothpick to a paper clip. Do you think the toothpick will attract (hold) the paper clip?

Prediction: _____

_____

Try it. What happened? _____

_____

Science

The Scientific Method

You can be a scientist and conduct your own experiment. Use this outline to plan your experiment.

Question
What is your question? _____

_____

Prediction
What do you think will happen? _____

_____

Steps
Write out your experiment steps and then try them.

1. _____

2. _____

3. _____

4. _____

Results
Tell what happened.

_____

_____

Conclusion
Why do you think that happened?

_____

_____

_____

Magnets in Everyday Life

Magnets are all around us. They are visible, as well as hidden, in our homes. There are magnets on or in our refrigerators. They are in can openers and on cabinet doors. A certain kind of magnet called an *electromagnet* operates many items in our homes.

An electromagnet is an iron object with wire wrapped around it wherein electricity is run through the wire and converts the iron object into a magnet by aligning the iron molecules in the object. Without electromagnets, we would not have televisions, lights, computers, telephones, and would not be able to start our cars and trucks.

Ask children to think about a world without magnets or electromagnets. What would that be like? How would life be different? If desired, you can try some experiments with electromagnetism. Several of the books listed in the Bibliography (page 79) have electromagnetic experiments in them: *Exploring Magnetism,* by Neil Ardley; *Electricity and Magnets,* by Barbara Taylor; and *Science Projects About Electricity and Magnetism,* by Robert Gardner.

Here is one experiment to get you started:

Materials

- large, steel nail
- a compass
- a switch
- a covered copper wire
- 6-volt battery
- paper clips

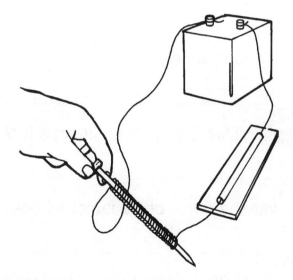

Directions

Test the nail with the compass to see if it magnetized. Wind the center of the wire around the nail 30 times *in the same direction.* Connect one end of the wire to the battery (make sure you connect the wire itself, not just the wire's covering); connect the opposite end to the switch. Connect the switch to the remaining battery terminal with another section of wire. Turn on the switch (by creating a connection) and wait a few seconds. Touch the nail to the paper clips. Is the nail now magnetic?

William Gilbert

William Gilbert was born in England in 1544. He was a medical doctor but became most famous for what he discovered about magnets.

He studied many legends about magnets. In the legends, natural rock magnets were called lodestones. He studied how the Earth acted like a natural magnet and made lodestones work like compasses. Without a good compass, sailing ships could be lost out at sea forever.

William Gilbert wrote a famous book called *De Magnete*, which is Latin for "on the magnet." It was published in 1600. He died in 1603.

1. When and where was William Gilbert born?

   _____

2. What is a lodestone?

   _____

3. What is William Gilbert most famous for?

   _____

4. What was the name of his famous book? What does the title mean?

   _____

5. When did William Gilbert die? How many years did he die after *De Magnete* was published?

   _____

54

Michael Faraday

Michael Faraday was a British scientist. He is well known for his studies of electromagnetics.

Use the activity below (and follow-up listening sheet, page 56) to help your children understand the basic concept of electromagnetism, as well as strengthen their listening skills. Explain to your children that they will be listening to information about a scientist named Michael Faraday and a magnet discovery that he made. Remind them to listen carefully in order to find out why he is famous. Read the information below to your children.

Michael Faraday was a scientist who lived in England two-hundred years ago. He discovered many ways to use electromagnets. Electromagnetics is the study of electricity and magnetism. When a wire is simply wrapped around an iron object it does not do anything special, but when electricity is switched on and the currents of electricity pass through the wire, a magnetic field is created. There is a difference between an electromagnet and a regular magnet. A regular magnet always keeps its magnetic force. An electromagnet can be switched on and off. When the electric current is turned on, there is a magnetic force. When the electric current is turned off, it no longer has a magnetic force. We use electromagnets in many ways. Telephones, computers, televisions, electric motors, cars, and even washing machines use electromagnets in order to work.

After reading the passage to your children, distribute individual copies of the listening sheet (page 56). Have each child complete the page with information he or she remembers from the passage. When the children have completed as much of the sheet as they can, have them pair up and work together to recall any information they may have missed. After a few more minutes, reread the passage of information to the children, encouraging them to fill in any missing answers.

Gather the children together as one large group and ask them what they discovered about the need to listen well. Ask them to share what they have discovered about working with a partner. Ask if they had some answers that their partners could not remember? Were their partners helpful in recalling information they forgot? Mention the phrase, *two heads are better than one*, to your children and ask them to tell you what they think this means. Remind your children that it is important to listen carefully, work well with others, and always be ready to help a friend in need (just as Michael Faraday helped us to live better!).

Did You Listen Carefully?

1. Who was Michael Faraday?

_____

2. Where was Michael Faraday from?

_____

3. When was he alive?

_____

4. What did he study?

_____

5. What is an electromagnet?

_____

6. How is a regular magnet different from an electromagnet?

_____

_____

7. What things do we have in our homes that use electromagnets?

_____   _____

_____   _____

_____   _____

Scientist Research

Choose a scientist that you would like to learn more about. Use this sheet to record what you have learned.

What is the name of your selected scientist?

_____

When was the scientist born?_____

Is he or she still alive? Yes_____ No _____

If not, when did he or she die? _____

Where did the scientist live as a child? As an adult?

_____

What did your scientist study?

_____

Why is he or she famous?

_____

What contributions did your scientist make to society?

_____

How would life be different without your scientist's discoveries or inventions?

_____

_____

Draw an illustration of your scientist and his or her famous discoveries or inventions on the back of this paper.

Name Magnets

Materials

- black construction paper

- adhesive business-card magnets (available at business-supply stores)

- scissors

- craft glue

- a small mixing bowl

- a variety of tempera paint colors

- a spoon

- small empty glue bottles

- a small towel

Preparation

1. Cut the black construction paper to fit the size of the business-card magnets.

2. Peel the paper off of the adhesive side of the magnets and attach the adhesive to the construction-paper cutouts; align the edges and trim, if necessary.

3. In a small bowl, mix 1/4 cup (60ml) of glue with a few drops of tempera paint; stir until well blended. Pour the glue into one of the small glue bottles.

4. Rinse out the mixing bowl with warm water. Dry the bowl with the small towel. Repeat step 3 to make several different colors of glue.

Directions

1. The children squeeze a series of dots using a chosen color of glue onto the construction paper magnets to write the letters in their first names.

2. The children then outline their magnets' edges with a contrasting color of glue dots. Allow the glue names and borders to dry thoroughly.

Refrigerator Magnets

Materials

- waxed paper
- salt dough (recipe below)
- tempera paint (various colors)
- paint brush
- small round magnets
- craft glue or glue gun

Directions

1. Cover the workspace with waxed paper.

2. Each refrigerator magnet will require a piece of salt dough about the size of a golf ball. Mold the dough into a desired shape.

3. Allow the shape to dry for several days to ensure dough is completely hardened. (Making a flat design or object shortens the drying time.)

4. Paint the shape with tempera paints; allow to dry.

5. Attach a magnet to the back of the shape using the craft glue or glue gun.

Salt Dough Recipe

- salt

- white flour

- water

- large, plastic self-sealing bag

Directions

1. In a mixing bowl, mix one part salt, two parts flour, and one part water. If the mixture seems too stiff, add a bit more water. If the mixture seems too soft, add a bit of flour. Knead the mixture until it reaches the consistency of bread dough.

2. Place the prepared salt dough in the self-sealing plastic bag so that the dough does not dry out.

Art

Make a Funny Face

See page 21, #4 for suggested use.

Magnetic Earth Art

The earth is a giant magnet. The magnetic field around it is called the *magnetosphere*. The magnetosphere makes a barrier around the earth. You can visually demonstrate the earth and its surrounding magnetic field with this art project.

Materials

- earth pattern (page 76)
- markers, crayons, or colored pencils
- 13" x 18" (12.5cm x 46 cm) sheet of black construction paper
- glitter (silver and/or gold)
- scissors
- glue (in a small-tipped glue bottle)
- pencil

Directions

1. Color and cut out the earth pattern. Glue the earth cutout to the center of the black construction paper.

2. Using a pencil, draw large ovals beginning from the center of the earth and extending beyond (see the illustration for placement). Trace over the "N" to indicate the North pole and the "S" to indicate the South pole.

3. Squeeze a trail of glue along the pencil-drawn lines. Sprinkle glitter onto the glue lines; shake off the excess glitter. Allow the project to dry before displaying.

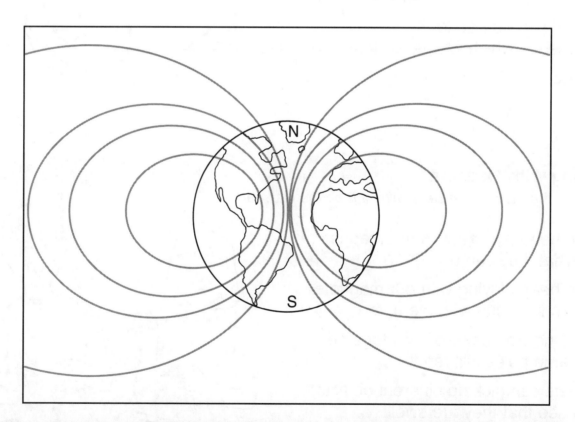

A Magnetic Idea: Have the children write a sentence or short paragraph explaining the concept of the earth being a natural magnet. Display the children's writings alongside their magnetic earth art in the hallway or library.

Magnet Songs

Little Magnet

(Sung to the tune of *Oh, Susannah*)

Well, I have this little magnet that I never want to lose,
It attracts so many things and it's just so fun to use.

Oh, little magnet, your force is very strong,
You can pick up pins and paper clips and make a chain so long.

Oh, little magnet, oh, won't you help me please?
I have too many things to do, you help do them with ease!

The Compass

(Sung to the tune of *Twinkle, Twinkle Little Star*)

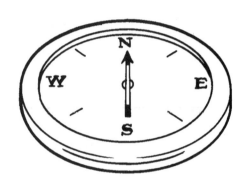

Compass, compass in my hand,
Guide me to some other land.

I look at you as I go forth,
Help me tell which way is North.

Compass, compass, I can tell,
You do your job very well.

Playing With Magnets

(Sung to the tune of *I've Been Working on the Railroad*)

We've been playing with our magnets,
See what they can do.

We've been playing with our magnets,
You can have fun with them, too.

North and South poles stick together,
The same poles will repel.

Magnets can pick up different objects,
You'll see that they are swell!

Write a Song

Fill in the blanks below to create your own songs about magnets.

(Sung to the tune of *Three Blind Mice*)

Magnets, magnets, magnets.

Magnets, magnets, magnets.

They are _____.

They are _____.

Magnets pick up _____.

Magnets stick to _____.

They can do so many things,

Magnets, magnets, magnets!

(Sung to the tune of *Mary Had a Little Lamb*)

If you have a mag-net, a mag-net, a mag-net,

If you have a mag-net,

_____.

Touch it to a _____, _____, _____.

Touch it to a _____, *(pause)*

and it will _____.
      (attract/repel)

Horseshoe Magnet Cookies

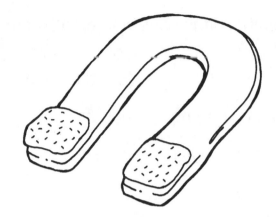

Ingredients

- sugar-cookie dough (use any basic recipe)

- baking parchment paper (cut into 4" x 4" [11cm x 11cm] squares)

- red icing (white icing colored with food coloring)

- chocolate candy sprinkles

To make a horseshoe magnet cookie, each child needs a golf-ball size portion of dough. The child rolls the dough into a rope, then places the rope in a horseshoe shape on a square sheet of parchment paper and presses it flat.

Place all of the children's cookies onto baking sheets and bake according to the chosen recipe. Allow the cookies to cool completely. Using the red frosting, each child ices *the ends only* of the horseshoe cookie and tops the icing with chocolate candy sprinkles (to mimic iron filings).

Magnetic Poles Tag

Getting Ready to Play

1. Using construction paper, make red shirt tags labeled "North" for half of the children. Make green shirt tags labeled "South" for the remaining children.

2. Attach one tag to the front of each child's shirt with a safety pin.

Playing the Game

1. Take the children to a large, open play area. Choose one child to be "it."

2. The child who is "it" tries to tag another child. If another child is tagged, he or she is now "it." To be "safe," and not be able to be tagged, a child must be standing back-to-back with another child who is wearing an *opposite* pole tag. For example, a child wearing a North-pole tag can stand back-to-back with a child wearing a South-pole tag. Two children with the same tags cannot stand together. Paired children can only be standing back-to-back "safe" for 10 seconds. Then they must run to find another opposite pole partner.

3. Play continues for a predetermined period of time.

Jumprope Rhymes

After reading the story, *Marta's Magnets* (page 5), share these jumprope rhymes from Joanna Cole's book *Miss Mary Mack and Other Children's Street Rhymes* (William Morrow and Company, 1990) with your children.

Number one, touch your tongue.
Number two, touch your shoe.
Number three, touch your knee.
Number four, touch the floor.
Number five, learn to jive.
Number six, pick up sticks.
Number seven, go to heaven.
Number eight, shut the gate.
Number nine, touch your spine.
Number ten, do it all again!

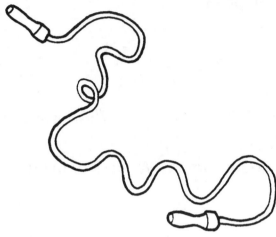

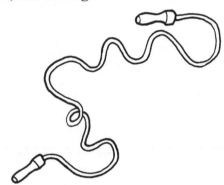

Hippity-hop to the barbershop
To buy a stick of candy.
One for you and one for me,
And one for sister Mandy.

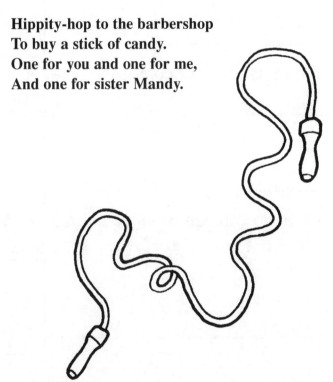

Oh, little playmate,
Come out and play with me.
And bring your dollies three.
Climb up my apple tree.
Slide down my rainbow,
Into my cellar door.
And we'll be jolly friends,
Forevermore, more, more.

So sorry, playmate,
I cannot play with you.
My dolly has the flu,
Boo-hoo, hoo-hoo, hoo-hoo.
I've got no rainbow.
I've got no cellar door
But we'll be jolly friends
Forevermore, more, more.

Have you ever, ever, ever
In your long-legged life
Seen a long-legged sailor
Kiss his long-legged wife?
No, I never, never, never,
In my long-legged life
Saw a long-legged sailor
Kiss his long-legged wife.

It's Compass Time!

Staying near your school building, answer the following questions using a compass.

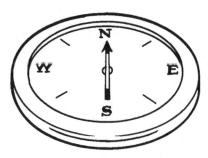

1. Find North. What are you facing? _____

2. Turn to the South. What do you see in front of you?

   Draw it.

   _____

3. Find East on your compass. What do you see?

   Draw it.

   _____

4. What do you see when you turn to the West?

   Draw it.

   _____

5. Try turning your compass in different directions. Does the North-pointing needle move or stay in the same place? Why does this happen?

   _____

6. With an adult, find the North side of your school building. On the back of this paper, draw a bird's eye view of your school building and label the North, South, East, and West walls. If you would like to, draw yourself standing next to the North wall.

Web Sites

Magnet Web Sites for Children

Bill Nye, the Science Guy's Nye Labs Online

http://nyelabs.kcts.org/

Your children will thoroughly enjoy this science Web site. The site contains excerpts from past television programs of Bill Nye, the Science Guy. Children can search the site to find information about magnetism and find links to other educational Web sites.

Electromagnets

http://howstuffworks.com/electromagnet.htm

This site shares basic information on how an electromagnet works and electromagnetism. You will also find a variety of experiments to try.

Kids Magnet Zone

http://www.mqii.com/kids.html

MagMan, this sites "main attraction," helps you understand "What is a Magnet?" and will link you to other sites. If you'd like to, you can talk (send a e-mail) to MagMan himself!

The Science Club

http://www.halcyon.com/sciclub/kidquest.html

Children can access a variety of scientists and ask them questions.

Virtual Science Fair

http://www.parkmaitland.org/sciencefair/index.html

This Web site shows children excellent examples of experiments done using the Scientific Method (Question, Prediction, Steps, Result, Conclusion). This site also highlights children's inventions.

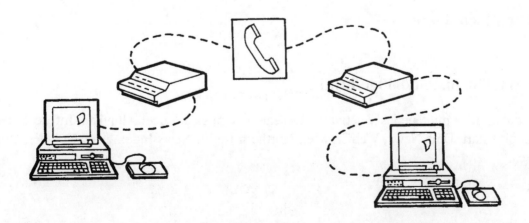

Web Sites *(cont.)*

General Science Web Sites for Teachers

The Magic School Bus
http://www.scholastic.com/magicschoolbus/

Join Ms. Friz and her gang as you explore what's happening on the PBS show, visit the Magic School Bus Art Gallery, find out when The Traveling Bus show will be in your area, and discover answers to the most frequently asked Magic School Bus questions.

National Science Foundation
http://www.nsf.gov

This Web site has information pertaining to the latest science news, grant information, and links to other science resources.

Teachers.Net
http://www.teachers.net/

This Web site is full of helpful resources for teachers. The lesson plans section contains magnet experiments, as well as other creative plans to use with your children. The site also contains a teacher chatboard, a live chatroom, and announcements about upcoming events for teachers.

Web Searches

Using a search engine is easy to do. Simply type in the Web search address (a few are listed below); then enter your selected keyword or keywords related to your topic.

Inference Find
http://infind.inference.com/infind/infind.exe

Lycos
http://www.lycos.com/

800go
http://www.800go.com/800go/html

This particular site simultaneously activates 12 search engines at once: Altavista, Infoseek, Home wiz, Excite, Look smart, Deja News, WebCrawler, Northern Light, News Index, MetaCrawler, Dog Pile, and Ask Jeeves.

A Magnetic Experience

Give your children the opportunity to show off their magnet expertise with this series of culminating activities. Invite parents, administrators, and other classes to join in the "magnetic" fun!

Centers

Assign two or three children to serve as scientists for each magnet experiment center. Arrange the room into station areas wherein the visiting guests can rotate through the stations. Some suggested experiments are: Are All Metals Magnetic? (page 16), Make a Magnet (page 17), Opposites Attract (page 18), Balancing Act (page 19), Line 'em Up (page 26), Make a Compass (page 27), Magnetic Fields (page 28), Iron Filings (page 29), Earth: A Giant Magnet (page 30), Hang On! (page 46), and Water Rescue (page 47).

Games

Encourages your guests to participate in one of the magnet races (pages 48-50). Have two of your children act as the games' referees.

Talk Show

Have your children prepare and perform a Magnet Talk Show (pages 70 and 71).

Music

Delight your guests with a group-sing using the magnet songs (page 62), as well as serenading them with your children's own made-up versions (page 63).

Treats

Have your children make a supply of Horseshoe Magnet Cookies (page 64) to serve to the guests as they arrive or give to them as they leave.

Souvenirs

Send off your guests with souvenir refrigerator magnets (page 59) and magnetic personality awards (page 78) as a remembrance of their "magnetic" experience!

Plan a Talk Show

Interviews

Choose a child (or have a try-out) to be the talk-show host. The host of the show will interview famous scientists who have studied magnetism as well as other special guests. Choose a child to be William Gilbert (page 54) and another to be Michael Faraday (page 55). Have these children (and a few "assistants") review the information learned about these two men. Assign another small group of children to write the interview questions for the host to ask these two famous scientists during the talk-show interviews.

Magnet Reports

Choose a few children to share reports they have written about magnets. These children may also want to share results and discoveries they have made while conducting magnet experiments.

Attractive Commercials

Assign another group of children to create commercials that advertise magnetic products, such as refrigerator magnets or magnetic can openers. Children participating in these commercials should think of ways to present the products to make them "attractive" to the audience.

Magnet Inventions

Have some children share their magnet inventions (If I Were a Scientist, page 35). If possible, have the children actually make their invented items to present to the talk-show audience.

Stage Props

Every talk-show set needs stage props. Assign several children to plan the appearance of the talk-show set. Have them decide on the furniture needed, the backdrop design, clothing, and announcement signs.

Advertising

Your talk show needs to be promoted! Children in the "advertising department" should decide how to promote the talk show. They may choose to create invitations to give or send to administrators, parents, or they may choose to do "live" promotional presentations to other classes inviting them to attend the show.

Talk-Show Format and Script

See page 71 for a sample talk-show script (as well as serving as a suggested format for the talk show).

Talk-Show Script

Good afternoon, ladies and gentlemen! My name is

_____ and welcome to
name of host

_____.
name of the talk show

Our first guest today is _____.
name of the famous scientist guest

(The host interviews the guest scientist with predetermined questions. If more than one interview will take place, after interviewing the first guest, the host introduces the next famous scientist guest and conducts the interview.)

We have some other special guests with us today. Our first special guest is

_____ who
name of guest

will be sharing _____.
a report or experiment results

(The host then introduces any additional special guests using the same format outlined above after each guest shares a report or experiment result.)

Thank you for sharing with us. Your work is very interesting! Well, audience, it's time for a word from our sponsors. Please stay tuned.

(Children involved in the commercials come out and perform.)

Welcome back! In this part of our show we have some guests who have interesting inventions to share with us.

(The inventors take turns sharing their drawings and/or actual inventions.)

Well folks, that's all the time we have for our show today. Before we go, we'd like you to meet some of our show's producers.

(Children involved in assisting the scientists, writing interview questions, designing stage props, and advertising the talk show introduce themselves to the audience.)

Thank you for joining us and have a "magnetic" day!

"Magnetic" Bulletin Boards

Which Things Are Magnetic?

Attach a variety of magnetic and nonmagnetic objects to a bulletin-board background using clear packaging tape. Items could include an empty soda and/or soup can, a pencil, a plastic cup, a wooden block, etc. Tie a long string to a strong magnet and tape the free end of the string to the board. To interact with the display, a child guesses whether or not an object is magnetic. The child then touches the magnet to the object to check his or her prediction.

Daily Response Graph

Attach bulletin-board paper to a magnetic surface such as a magnetic chalkboard or white board. Draw a yes/no graph on the background. Label a sentence strip with a question and attach it above the graph. Obtain small, head-shot photographs of each child and attach a small strip of self-sticking magnetic tape to the back of each one. Place the magnetic photos around the edge of the prepared graph. Each day the children read, or have read to them, a new "the question of the day" (written on a sentence strip) and place their photos appropriately on the yes/no graph.

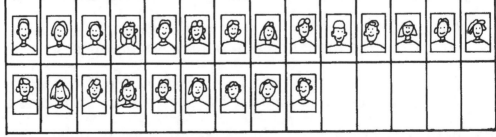

"Magnetic" Bulletin Boards *(cont.)*

Great Minds...

After your children research their selected scientists (page 57), have them rewrite the gained information in report form and display their research reports and illustrations.

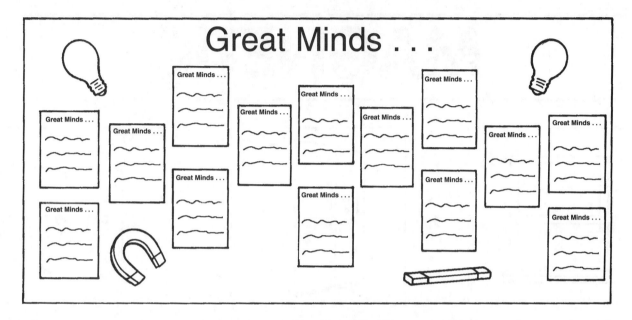

Is It or Isn't It?

Duplicate, enlarge, color, and cut out the magnet words and items (page 74). Divide a covered bulletin board in half with string; label one side *magnetic*, the other side *nonmagnetic*. As a participatory lesson, have the children indicate on which side the cutout items should be placed. For an extension, have the children create their own pictures of magnetic and nonmagnetic items and add them to the bulletin board.

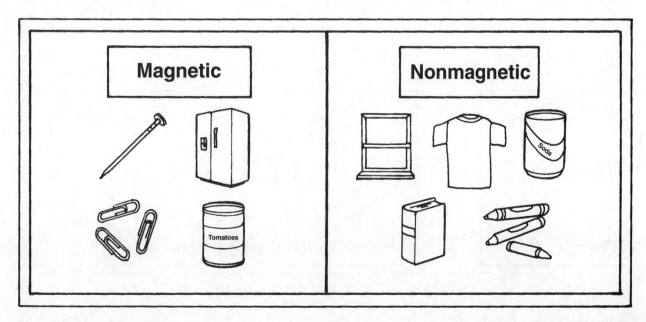

Magnetic Patterns

NONMAGNETIC

MAGNETIC

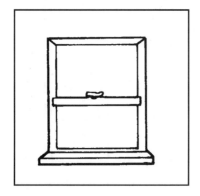  

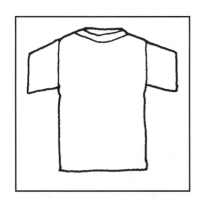 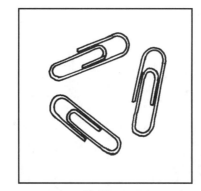 

Science Journal

I've learned that...

I've been wondering about...

Here's a picture of something I did.

Awards

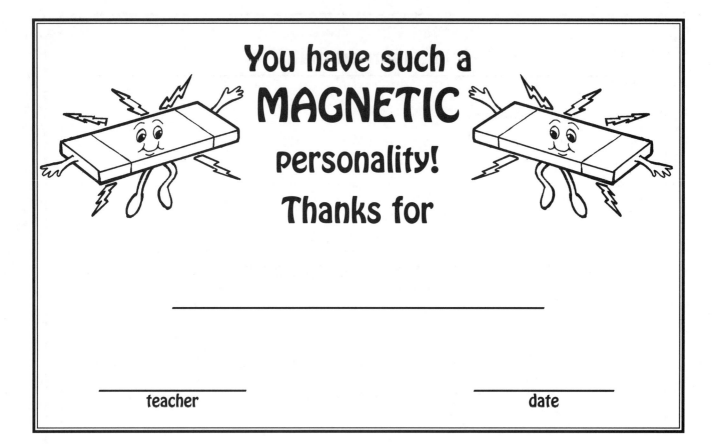

You have such a
MAGNETIC
personality!
Thanks for

_____

_____   _____
teacher   date

I can see
you are
ATTRACTED
to excellent work in

_____

_____   _____
teacher   date

Bibliography

Fiction

Fox, Mem. *Wilfrid Gordon McDonald Partridge*. Kane/Miller Book Publishers, 1985.

Heine, Helme. *Friends*. Aladdin, 1986.

Pfeffer, Wendy. *Marta's Magnets*. Silver Press, 1995.

Pfister, Marcus. *The Rainbow Fish*. Scholastic, 1992.

Silverstein, Shel. *The Giving Tree*. HarperCollins, 1964.

Nonfiction

Ardley, Neil. *Exploring Magnetism*. Franklin Watts Ltd., 1983.

Branley, Franklyn M. *What Makes a Magnet?* HarperCollins, 1996.

Cash, Terry and Barbara Taylor. *Fun with Science: Electricity and Magnets*. Warwick Press, 1989.

Challand, Helen J. *A New True Book: Experiments with Magnets*. Children's Press, 1986.

Cooper, Jason. *Science Secrets Discovery Library: Magnets*. The Rourke Corporation, 1992.

Fowler, Allan. *Rookie Read-About Science: What Magnets Can Do*. Children's Press, 1995.

Gardner, Robert. *Science Projects about Electricity and Magnetism*. Enslow Publishers., 1994.

Gibson, Gary. *Science for Fun: Playing with Magnets*. Millbrook Press, 1995.

Jennings, Terry. *Junior Science: Magnets*. Franklin Watts, 1990.

Krensky, Stephen. *All About Magnets*. Scholastic, 1992.

Santrey, Laurence. *Magnets*. Troll, 1985.

Taylor, Barbara. *Science Starters: Electricity and Magnets*. Franklin Watts, 1990.

Van Cleave, Janice P. *Magnets: Mind-boggling Experiments You Can Turn into Science Fair Projects*. John Wiley and Sons, 1993.

Magnet Book and Kit

Usbourne Kids Kit. This kit includes a *Science with Magnets* book, coated wire, two corks, paper clips, a nail, a horseshoe and bar magnet, clay, and a compass. Usborne books/kits are available at most bookstores, or try *www.amazon.com* if you are Internet-accessible.

Magnet Resources

Dowling Resources. 1-800-*MAGNET*-1. A "magnetic" supermarket of supplies including magnetic wands; giant horseshoe, ring, and bar magnets; iron filings; magnetic balls and chips; and much, much more.

Answer Key

Page 37

1. True

2. False–A compass is an instrument used to determine directions.

3. True

4. False– A magnetic pole is the strongest point on a magnet.

5. True

6. False–The magnets will stick together.

7. True

Page 41

1. 4

2. 7

3. 6

4. 5

5. 17

6. 9

Answer to Riddle: **A MAGNET**

Page 51

1. The magnet will attract the paper clip even in water.

2. The toothpick will not become magnetic because it has no iron in it.

Page 54

1. 1544; England

2. A lodestone is a natural, magnetic rock.

3. Writing a book about magnets.

4. *De Magnete*; on the magnet

5. 1603; 3 years

Page 56

1. Michael Faraday was a scientist.

2. England

3. About two hundred years ago.

4. He studied electromagnets and electromagnetism.

5. An electromagnet is a wire-wrapped, iron object that is made magnetic by sending electrical currents through the wire.

6. A regular magnet always has magnetic force. An electromagnet needs an active electric current flowing to make it magnetic.

7. Telephones, computers, televisions, electric motors, cars, and washing machines.